CLOSER LOOK AT

TIGERS, DOLPHINS,

KOALAS AND OTHER MAMMALS

Joyce Pope

Franklin Watts

LONDON ● SYDNEY

© Aladdin Books Ltd 1998
Designed and produced by
Aladdin Books Ltd
28 Percy Street
London W1P 0LD

*First published in Great Britain
in 1998 by*
Franklin Watts
96 Leonard Street
London EC2A 4RH

A catalogue record for this book is available
from the British Library.

ISBN: 0 7496 3224 0

Editor
Michael Flaherty

Designer
Jeff Gurney

Picture Research
Brooks Krikler Research

Front cover illustration
Gary Edgar-Hyde

Certain illustrations have appeared in
earlier books created by Aladdin Books.

The consultant Jane Parker gained her zoology degree
and then went to work at London Zoo to study the
reproductive biology of rare mammals. For the last
12 years she has been involved in writing books on
wildlife and science subjects.

Printed in Belgium

CONTENTS

INTRODUCTION

Mammals are the animals that we know best, largely because humans are mammals. Our pet cats and dogs are mammals. More unusual mammals include rhinos, dolphins and platypuses. There are about 4,000 different kinds of mammal and few places in the world where an explorer would not find them. Though most live in warm climates, they have become adapted to live in all sorts of places, including the Arctic and even the sea.

Mammals have a bony skeleton. Because of this, scientists call mammals "vertebrates" – along with fishes, amphibians, reptiles and birds. Mammals have lungs to breathe air, and are warm-blooded. Mammal mothers feed their babies on milk. They keep warm with a coat of fur or hair, or with a special kind of fat called blubber just under the skin.

WHAT ARE

INSIDE A MAMMAL

All mammals are clever animals, with a large brain. The spinal cord, protected by the bones of the back, takes and coordinates messages from the brain to the body. Blood is pumped round the body by the heart, taking oxygen from the lungs to the muscles and organs. Most mammals give birth to large babies that grow inside their mother's body until they are ready to be born.

Egg layers

The platypus (above) and the spiny anteater, or echidna, are the only two kinds of mammals that lay eggs. When the eggs hatch, the blind, helpless babies are fed on milk, like all other mammals. The mother platypus does not have teats, but the milk oozes from pores on her skin.

Brain

Young in the womb

Spinal cord

Lungs

Heart

ON CLOSER INSPECTION
– Air-breathers

Mammals, like all land animals, get their oxygen from the air. Even sea-living mammals, like this grey whale (right), still have to come to the surface to breathe, though they may be able to hold their breath for over an hour while they hunt underwater.

MAMMALS

Human skeleton
Compare the skeleton of a human being (right) with that of a horse (below). We walk upright and have no external tail, but we have the same basic structure. The easiest differences to spot are in our legs. We have five toes and walk on the whole length of our rather short feet. Horses run on the tip of one toe and increase the length of their stride with their very long foot and toe bones.

MAMMAL SKELETONS

All land mammals have similar skeletons. The skull protects the brain and, with the lower jaw, contains the teeth. All, except for sloths, have seven bones in their necks – giraffes, shrews and humans are all alike in this. Attached to the vertebrae (or backbones) are the ribs, which protect the lungs and the heart. The hip bones are also attached to the vertebrae but the shoulder blade is not. Mammals' leg bones are all made on the same pattern and the joints work in the same way. There is one large bone at the top of the leg, a pair of bones below this, then wrist or ankle bones, then hand or foot bones.

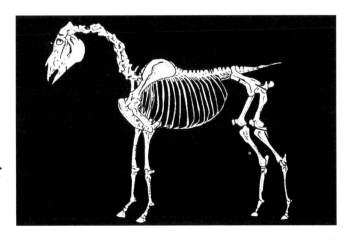

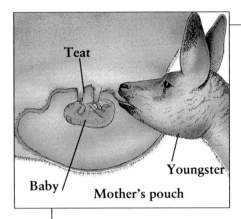

Teat

Youngster

Baby

Mother's pouch

Kangaroo

The smallest mammal babies are born to marsupials, or pouched mammals. They develop for a very short time inside their mothers' bodies. Once born they crawl to a pouch on their mother's belly.

Rearing a family is one of the most important things in any animal's life. In many mammals the female cares for her offspring alone, while in some both parents share the duties of rearing the young. In a few, mostly long-lived mammals, a family group jointly brings up the next generation.

CARING FOR

WOLVES

Wolves were among the most widespread of mammals until humans began to kill them. One reason for their success was their highly developed family life. Each group, or pack, of wolves occupies a home range, which overlaps the ranges of other packs, but which contains a territory that belongs to the family alone. In the pack normally only the dominant female produces cubs in any one year. She alone can give them milk, but once they have left the den, all the pack helps to protect them and bring them food (left). They also teach the cubs skills that will help them to hunt. As a result, wolf cubs grow up as part of a group, the members of which all depend on each other.

ON CLOSER INSPECTION – *Elephants*

A baby elephant, or calf, is born into a family group where all the adults are related females. There are always plenty of playmates, from newborn calves to 12-year olds. Calves will be cared for mostly by their mother, though aunts will help to guard them.

THEIR YOUNG

GREVY'S ZEBRAS

The closely-striped Grevy's zebras (below) live in dry country and only come together in small groups probably because of the lack of food. Males fight for territories through which they allow females and foals to pass. If a female is ready, the territory holder will mate with her. Stallions and mares remain in separate groups even after mating.

CHIMPANZEES

An important difference between humans, our close relatives the chimpanzees and other mammals is that humans and chimps take far longer to grow up than other animals do. This is because both human and chimpanzee children have a lot to learn in order to be able to look after themselves and function properly in their complex societies. Young chimps are dependent on their mothers for seven or eight years. Young humans are dependent on their mothers for about 14 years, almost twice as long.

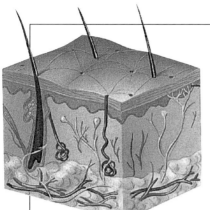

Skin and hair
Most mammals keep warm with a coat of hair. Each hair grows from deep in the skin (above) and helps to trap an insulating blanket of air round the animal's body.

Mammals are warm-blooded animals; their body temperature remains the same whatever the temperature of their surroundings. Their body chemistry works at a constant rate, so that they can be active even in cool places. Cold-blooded animals, such as reptiles, can only be active in warm places.

TEMPERATURE

FEEDING AND TEETH

To keep themselves warm and active, mammals need a great deal of food. They have evolved different kinds of teeth depending on their diet. Incisors are peg-like front teeth used for cutting or biting. Pointed canine teeth are for gripping and tearing. Cheek teeth, called molars, are for chewing or cutting food before swallowing. Not all mammals have all the different kinds of teeth. Some mammals, like anteaters or blue whales,

TIGER SKULL

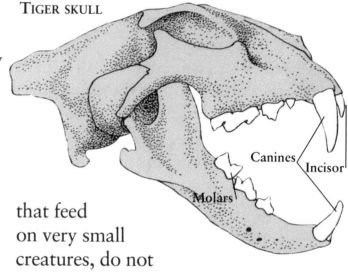

Canines
Incisor
Molars

that feed on very small creatures, do not need to chew their food, and have no teeth. Flesh eaters, like tigers (above), have nipping incisor teeth, tearing canine teeth, and, most important, slicing molar teeth, which cut their food into bite-sized pieces. Plant eaters, like horses (left), often lack canines. They cut grass with large incisors, and grind it up with big, flat-topped molar teeth. Dolphins have many peg-like teeth used only to hold their prey.

HORSE SKULL

Incisor

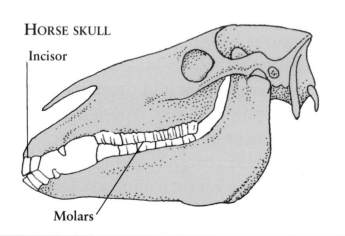

Molars

In winter when there isn't much food, a few small mammals, like the dormouse (right), go into a deep sleep called hibernation. Their heartbeat and breathing slow and their temperature drops to save energy until spring.

CONTROL

MAMMALS MOVING

When they are moving slowly, most mammals walk or trot, putting one fore- and one hindlimb forward at the same time and swinging their backs slightly from side to side. Their high body temperature allows them to move faster when they need to. When running, some mammals gallop. A galloping mammal bounds along using its front feet and its hind feet together. Its back acts like a spring as it is squeezed and stretched. The cheetah can gallop faster than all other mammals – about 100 kph. As these drawings show (below), it has a very flexible back. But even animals like horses, with quite stiff backs, gallop at up to 60 kph.

Feeding

Keeping a high body temperature needs a lot of fuel, or food. Plant-eating mammals are called herbivores. Most feed on a lot of different leaves. But the koala (below) feeds on only tender leaves from a few kinds of Eucalyptus trees. Some mammals are flesh eaters, or carnivores. Omnivores, like humans, bears and rats, eat almost anything.

Excitement

Fear

Anger

Joy

Sadness

Expressions

Animals that live in groups communicate with each other. They may use sounds, but body language and facial expressions, like these chimp expressions (above), are more often used. The position of the lips, whether or not the teeth are shown, or the eyes are open or closed all give information.

An animal finds out about its surroundings through its senses. The mammal's five main senses are sight, hearing, smell, taste and touch. Most mammals rely greatly on smell to find food, detect enemies and to communicate. Monkeys, apes and people rely more on sight and have good colour vision.

SENSES AND

TOOL USERS

The most complex behaviour is found in intelligent, social animals. Chimpanzees, which are some of the cleverest mammals, live in groups where each one constantly reacts with others. If a senior member of the group makes a discovery, the others quickly take advantage of it. They are among the few animals that use tools. Another tool-user is the sea otter (below) of the North Pacific Ocean. While floating on its back, it cracks shellfish open on a stone that it holds against its chest.

On Closer Inspection
– *Mammal supersense*

Some mammals that hunt in the dark, such as bats and dolphins (below), make high-pitched squeaks. They can hear the echo bouncing back from anything in the stream of sound, like a submarine's sonar. This is called echolocation.

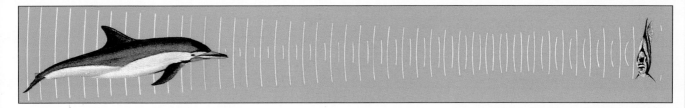

BEHAVIOUR

SHARP EYES

The sharp eyes of zebras give warning of danger and the herd takes flight when a pride of lions is on the prowl. Zebras are family animals and use their eyes to recognise members of their own group, for every one has a slightly different pattern of stripes. Although their eyesight is very sharp, they do not see things in colour as we (and chimpanzees) do. Instead, everything is in shades of grey, with perhaps a faint tinge of colour.

Night sight & whiskers

The big eyes of the cuscus (above) gather all the light in its New Guinea forest home as it searches for food at night. Unlike many animals active at night, it does not have large, sensitive ears to tell it of the movement of other creatures. Instead, the long whiskers round its snout and by its eyes are part of its sense of touch and help it to scramble safely.

Slothful sloth

Sloths live up to their name; they are the most inactive animals. Three-toed sloths (above) rarely move more than 38 m in a day. They usually live in and feed on Cecropia trees.

Brazilian tapir

The Brazilian tapir lives on the ground, rarely far from water, where it takes refuge if chased. It hides during the day, but comes out at night to feed on plants (below). Like most tropical forest animals, it is becoming rarer and is now on the list of endangered species.

orests are rich in mammals. A few large forest-dwellers, like deer and tapirs, live all their lives at ground level, but many others, like squirrels and monkeys, move up and down in the trees. Most of them are agile, fast-moving creatures, able to perform amazing acrobatic feats as a matter of daily life. Only a few, like sloths, lead a slow life.

FOREST

HIGH SWINGERS

Moving fast among the branches is dangerous, so forest mammals have to be able to grip firmly to prevent themselves from falling. One way that they do this is to have claws that dig into the bark. Squirrels use this method of hanging on. They cannot hold the smallest twigs, but they are able to climb up and down the vertical trunks of trees. The other way, used by monkeys and apes, is to have hands and feet with one or more toes that fold across the others, called opposable toes, so the creature can grasp even the smallest branches. Koalas have opposable fingers and toes and big claws as well!

Gibbons and some monkeys swing along the branches by their hands, a way of moving through the trees that is called brachiation. Gibbons are so agile that they can even walk a tightrope (left).

ON CLOSER INSPECTION
– Camouflage in forests

Many forest-living mammals have fur that is blotched with colour, usually black or dark brown on a yellowish background, like this jaguar. This breaks up the outline of their bodies so that they are almost impossible to see in the dappled light of the forest.

DWELLERS

Tarsier jumping

Tarsiers' bodies are about the size of a grapefruit, but their long legs enable them to jump about two metres (below). Each toe ends in a friction pad, which enables the animal to land and cling onto the vertical trunk of trees with rough or smooth bark.

NIGHT LIFE

Forests may be gloomy places, even in daytime, but some animals wait until after nightfall before they become active. Most of these feed on night insects, but some, like nectar-feeding bats, rely on trees that only open their flowers after dark. Moving quietly among the branches is tricky. Animals, such as the tarsier, use their huge ears and eyes to detect food and avoid obstructions.

The chase

Meat eaters that live on the plains stalk as close as they can to their sharp-eyed prey before giving chase. The cheetah is the fastest of all mammals and can reach a speed of up to 100 kph very quickly, though it rarely runs for more than 200m at this speed.

The majority of the world's large mammals live on open plains. They mostly live in herds and do not stay in the same place for long, but travel slowly, grazing fresh grass as they go. When they return to their starting place, the plants, fertilised by their droppings, are growing strongly again.

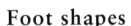

Foot shapes

Zebra and antelopes stand on the tips of their toes, so that the bones of their feet increase the length of their stride as they run. Big mammals like rhinos and elephants have more but shorter toes, which spread to carry their weight.

Horse   Pronghorn

Rhinoceros   Elephant

OPEN PLAINS

Grasses, which are eaten by most large animals, are newcomers among plants. They were not widespread until about 30 million years ago, but once the plains were covered with grasses, many kinds of animals evolved rapidly to use the new food source. This picture (right) shows an early ancestor of the elephants, some gigantic, long-necked relatives of the horse, and ancient gazelles. These gazelles were the most important, for they developed a new sort of digestive system for dealing with grass. They regurgitated the grass they'd already eaten to chew it again. This is called chewing the cud and today most large herbivores are cud chewers.

ON CLOSER INSPECTION
– *Aardvark*

The aardvark is about the size of a pig. It uses its big claws to tear open the nests of ants or termites, which are its main food. It scoops up the insects on its sticky tongue, which is up to 45 cm long. It lives in a large burrow.

IN THE OPEN

Feeding levels

Animals can live together on the African savannahs because each uses a separate part of the environment, eating different plants and browsing different levels of the trees that grow along watercourses. The giraffe and elephant reach the highest, while the gerenuk stands on its hind legs to browse the lower branches of trees.

ARCTIC LANDS

The windswept tundras of the Arctic are home to such mammals as lemmings, Arctic hares and foxes, wolverines and reindeer. Most reindeer migrate to more sheltered places for the winter. This reindeer (above) lives in Spitsbergen and cannot escape from its island home, so before winter arrives it feeds on the flowering heads of grasses to give it energy for the coming season.

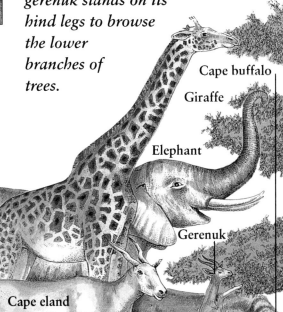

Cape buffalo

Giraffe

Elephant

Gerenuk

Zebra Wildebeest

Rhino

Cape eland

Impala

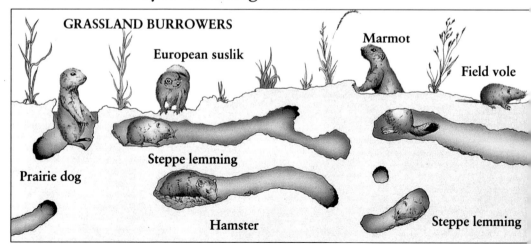

Wombats

The wombat (above) is an Australian pouched mammal, closely related to the koala. It is one of the largest burrowers, with a head and body length of about a metre and an average weight of 25kg. In its territory it may have several burrows up to 20 metres long. During the daytime it rests in one of these, but at night it comes out to feed on grasses.

Burrowing rodents

Many kinds of mouse-like rodents, such as the field vole, make shallow burrows among the roots of grasses or the surface soil, though hamsters burrow deeper. The champion rodent burrowers are ground squirrels such as prairie dogs or marmots.

Small mammals often shelter from the weather and their enemies by living in burrows. Some, such as moles and mole rats, spend all their lives underground. Others, such as rabbits, come out to find food on the surface. Some burrowers live alone, but many live in family groups. Prairie dogs, live in groups so large that they are called "townships".

BURROWING

GOING UNDERGROUND

Most small mammals, such as rabbits, make a burrow by digging with their front paws and kicking the loose earth away with their hind feet. Grasslands can benefit from burrow-making, which brings fresh soil to the surface of the ground. Many burrows have several entrances to aid escape from enemies. Farmers dislike burrowing animals. Cattle and horses may break their legs in burrows and machinery can get stuck in them, so in many parts of the world burrowing animals have been destroyed on a large scale.

GRASSLAND BURROWERS

European suslik

Marmot

Field vole

Prairie dog

Steppe lemming

Hamster

Steppe lemming

ON CLOSER INSPECTION
– *Food stores*

Animals' burrows usually contain an area for storing food. Hamsters have pouches in the side of their mouths which they cram with grain to carry back to their larders (right). The common hamster may make a larder containing up to 10kg of food.

MAMMALS

WINTER SHELTER

Burrows in snow provide shelter for some animals against the low temperatures and howling winds of the far north. The biggest of these are female polar bears, which make a den by tunnelling through snow packed against a steep slope (right). This burrow is several metres long and ends in one or more rooms. The entrance to the burrow is often blocked by snow, but the bear may make a ventilation hole in the roof of her resting place. Snugly away from the cold outside world, the bear sleeps through the winter and even produces her cubs at this time.

Woodchucks
The woodchuck (above) hibernates in a long, deep burrow and does not emerge until spring is well under way.

More than a quarter of all known mammals are bats. Bats are the only mammals that have powerful wings capable of true flight, but many other mammals glide like paper darts for long distances. Usually they are forest canopy animals that avoid the perils of the ground by taking great leaps from one tree trunk to another.

TAKING TO

Night flight

All bats are nocturnal – active at night. A few species eat fish, nectar or fruit, or even blood, but most catch night-flying insects. They find their food by echolocation (see page 13). While in flight they send out high-pitched squeaks all the time. This supplies them constantly with new information about their surroundings. The flaps of skin that decorate the faces of many kinds of bats probably help in concentrating the beam of sounds. Bats' wing membranes contain elastic fibres, so when they are not in flight the wings contract and fold away. This stops them from getting in the way as the animal moves about.

HIGH FLYERS

Bats fly by flapping their wings. This picture (below) shows how the wing is formed of a soft skin, supported by the slender arms and hugely elongated hand and finger bones. At the rear, the wing is attached to the ankle and is pulled taut by small movements of the leg, so bats use both fore- and hindlimbs in flight. The membrane between the hind-limbs and the tail is often used as a pouch for catching or holding insects. Bat flight tends to look fluttery and weak, but bats can hover and fly with great precision.

Bats can fly fast: the top speed is about 80 kph, and some bats fly strongly enough to make migrations of over 1000 km.

ON CLOSER INSPECTION – *The colugo*

One of the strangest of gliding mammals is the lemur-like colugo of Southeast Asia, which has a membrane that stretches from the sides of its head round its limbs to the end of its tail (right). With this, it can cover distances of over 100 m between trees.

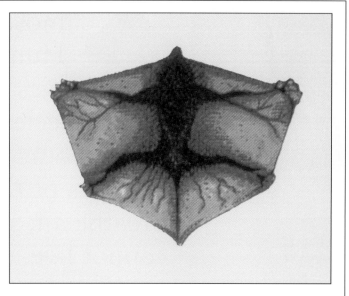

THE AIR

GLIDING POSSUM

There are no true squirrels in Australia, but gliding possums (below), which are pouched animals, live much like flying squirrels in other warm parts of the world. These little creatures are active at night, leaping and gliding up to 100m in their search for nectar, or buds or insects. One has been seen catching an insect in flight, though it does not use echolocation.

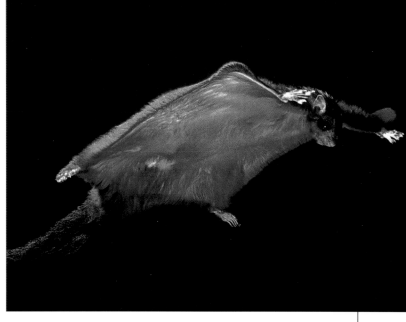

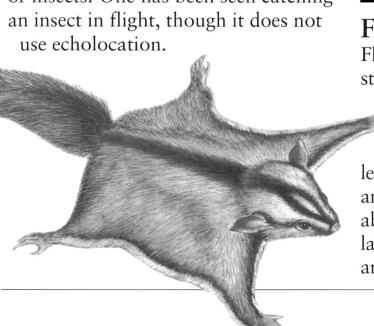

FLYING SQUIRRELS

Flying squirrels have a flap of skin that stretches between their fore- and hind-limbs. The spotted giant flying squirrel (above) lives high in the forests of Southeast Asia. When leaping between trees it spreads its limbs and glides, even as much as 450 m. It is able to curve, or bank, in flight. Before landing, it brings its hind feet forwards and up, so very little height is lost overall.

A lmost all mammals can swim. Humans and apes are the only ones that cannot do so naturally. Many species take refuge from enemies in water. Some live most or all of their lives in rivers or the oceans. But they must all breathe air, so even the best swimmers cannot live underwater all the time.

WATERY

Weight in water

Because water is much denser than air, it supports the bodies of the animals that live in it. As a result, many of the creatures that live in water are large and heavy-bodied. On land hippos (above) may be slow and ungainly. But underwater film has shown that in water even they look light-limbed and elegant.

SWIMMING

Otters, beavers and platypuses spend much of their time in water and have thick waterproof fur and webbed feet, which they use as paddles. Seals, manatees and dolphins keep warm with a layer of fat called blubber, which lies just below the skin. Their limbs are transformed into flippers, which are not suitable for walking or running.

Otter

Beaver

Dolphin

Platypus

Manatee

ON CLOSER INSPECTION
– Bubble nets

Humpback whales sometimes blow bubbles of air round a school of small fish (right). As the air bubbles rise to the surface of the water, they make a sort of net that the fish are afraid to go through. Then the whale rushes in to feed.

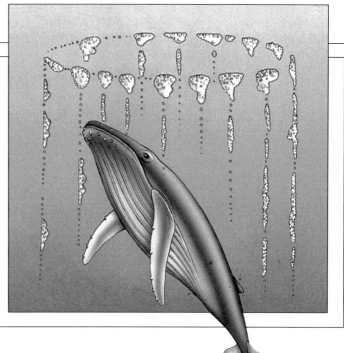

WORLDS

Food underwater

A few mammals, like beavers, that live in fresh water eat plants, but most aquatic mammals are carnivores. This elephant seal (below) feeds on fish and squid, which it often catches at depths of 250 m. The average length of time for a dive is about 20 minutes, though it may be much longer. Larger fish-eating whales, such as sperm whales, dive as deep as 350 m and hold their breath for even longer, as they hunt giant squid.

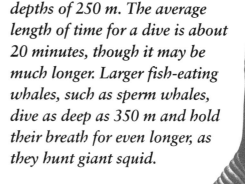

UNDERWATER GIANTS

The largest mammals are the great whales (below). These giants spend all their life in the ocean and die if they are washed ashore. Their huge, streamlined bodies have no fur and they swim with up and down movements of their tail flukes. They have no hindlimbs and their front legs are flippers, which are used mainly for balance and steering in the water.

Desert surfaces

The stony tundra in this picture (above) looks totally inhospitable, but lichens grow on the stones, and in places tiny flowering plants find shelter. Reindeer wander across, getting a little food from them. Large mammals in deserts always have to travel to find food. The reindeer's hooves spread to carry its weight over boggy ground. Camels' feet (below) have large pads on the underside, which are good for walking over sandy or gravelly deserts.

H uman beings are able to live in more places than any other mammals – we are even exploring space. Yet some mammals can live in environments so hostile that we can only make them bearable with the use of modern technology. Searing-hot deserts and cold Arctic wilderness areas are home to animals adapted to live in such extremes.

SURVIVING

HOT AND COLD DESERTS

Small mammals that live in either intense heat or cold escape the worst of the climate by living in burrows where they are protected against extremes. Hot-desert animals often close their burrows to keep them humid. They often have huge ears, like the fennec fox. These act like radiators to get rid of excess heat. In extremely cold places mammals, like the Arctic fox, have tiny ears and tails, which helps to keep the heat in. Animals that don't dig burrows often have very thick fur that insulates them against heat and cold.

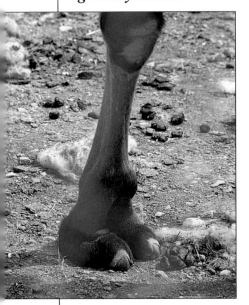

Fennec fox

Arctic and fennec foxes are related, but their ears tell us which one lives in the heat and which one in the cold.

Arctic fox

ON CLOSER INSPECTION
– *The longest sleep*

The small ground squirrels of central North America and Asia are active for less than three months each year. They sleep, or aestivate, in burrows when food is scarce during the hot summer and then sleep, or hibernate, during the difficult, cold winter months.

EXTREMES

ARCTIC GIANTS

Musk oxen (below) are the largest animals in the Arctic, ranging from Alaska to Greenland. In winter they move from lowland areas to higher ground, where the wind sweeps snow away from what little food there is. Their long outer fur overlies a fine inner coat so dense that the coldest winds and frosts cannot penetrate it.

Kangaroo rat

Mouse-like animals, such as the kangaroo rat (above), that live in open, sandy, hot deserts often have very big hind legs with long toes. These enable them to move fast across the sand, leaping like tiny kangaroos. They are among the animals best adapted to live in hot deserts. They come out of their burrows at night to feed on seeds and insects, but they hardly ever drink. They get enough water from the food they eat. Their kidneys work at least four times better than ours do, so they excrete very little liquid. This helps them retain as much liquid as possible from their diet.

House mice
A few small mammals that, like us, are capable of eating almost anything, have discovered that humans can provide them with food and shelter. House mice, brown rats and black rats often live uninvited in buildings and have become serious pests, spreading diseases as well as destroying stores of many kinds.

Sheepdogs
Our greatest partnership with another mammal is with dogs. Traditionally they guard property, herd flocks and act as companions. Now they are used to help the disabled and to find lost or hidden people, goods or drugs.

Human beings are the most abundant large mammals in the world. Our effect on all life is far greater than that of any other creature. We have used and, in many cases, abused the mammals that share the planet with us. In some cases, we have domesticated and enslaved other animals, though, in a few instances, they have become our partners.

IN THE

WHALING

In ancient times humans hunted other animals for their food. Nowadays that is not necessary for most people, but some wild animals are still hunted on a commercial scale. The one that causes most upset to many people is whaling. The great whale herds of the world were very nearly destroyed, with great cruelty, during the last century and the early part of this one. Today only Norway and Japan wish to continue commercial whaling. Because of their greatly reduced populations, there is some hope that even small-scale whale hunting, such as in this picture (right), will cease. Then the oceans can be made into whale reserves as some nations have proposed.

Foxes learned long ago that humans could provide them with food, such as chickens from farms. So they were hunted wherever possible. In recent years, foxes have made a new discovery – people's dustbins often contain food. Now there are more foxes in some towns than in the country.

HUMAN WORLD

DOMESTICATION

Most domestic animals such as cattle, pigs, elephants and camels have served us by carrying our burdens and providing us with meat, milk or leather. With horses there has been more of a partnership, partly because horses were important to conquering armies through the ages. Now they have been largely replaced by machines, in much of the world, but still have a role to play in cattle ranching and sports, such as horse racing.

Horses such as these shires (below) were bred to carry knights in armour. Now they work on farms.

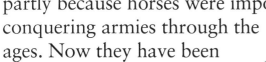

Extinction

An animal species becomes extinct when the last one of that kind of creature dies. Animals eventually become extinct in the natural course of events. But many have been made extinct because of human activity. Today, we are driving many species to the edge of extinction, often because they conflict with our interests. The picture (below) shows kangaroos, destined to be used as pet food. In the first half of the twentieth century great numbers of kangaroos were slaughtered, bringing some close to extinction. Today, they are protected by law and have recovered well.

As humans have increased in numbers, taking up more of the world, so other animals have been squeezed out of their living spaces. In ancient times mammals became rare through hunting. Nowadays many mammals are in danger of extinction because their habitats are being polluted and destroyed by our activities.

MAMMALS IN

TIGERS

At the turn of the century there were thought to be about 100,000 tigers across Asia. Now there are probably fewer than 7,000. They have died out in many places because they were hunted for their beautiful skins. People killed the wild animals that were the tiger's food, then killed the tigers when they ate cattle. Their habitat has been destroyed for its valuable timber and farmland. Tigers are still killed because some people imagine that their bones make good medicine. Perhaps in 100 years' time there may be some tigers in zoos, but at the present rate of destruction it is not likely that any will survive in the wild.

ON CLOSER INSPECTION
– *Symbol of conservation*

The giant panda is one of the rarest mammals in the world. It is the logo of the Worldwide Fund For Nature, one of the most important conservation groups. Such groups remind us that a world that is healthy for other animals is healthy for us too.

DANGER

Accidental death

Sometimes huge numbers of mammals are killed accidentally. At sea, whales, dolphins (below) and seals get caught in nearly invisible seine nets or tangled up in monofilament lines and drown. These nets and lines are being outlawed in Europe, but it will take a total ban to protect sea mammals the world over.

PROTECTING MAMMALS

Many mammals are now protected by international laws. But it is not enough to say that a creature must not be killed; it must also have the right sort of living space. European beavers (above), which were once common, became very rare by the end of the last century. Now their numbers are increasing as they are reintroduced into parts of Europe, such as in Poland and Russian Lapland.

MAMMAL RECORDS and AMAZING FACTS

The fastest humans can run 200 m at over 35 kph.

Shrews are fierce fighters and may attack animals bigger than themselves.

LARGEST
The biggest living mammal, now or ever, is the blue whale. The biggest one measured was 33.59 m in length. The heaviest one weighed 190 tonnes.

SMALLEST
The smallest land mammal is Savi's pygmy shrew. The head and body length of an adult is less than 35 mm and it weighs up to 2 g. The pygmy shrew found in western Europe (above) is slightly larger.

LONG DISTANCE
The pronghorn antelope of North America is the fastest land animal over long distances. Over 0.8 km it can run at 88.5 km/h. Over 6 km it can run at 56 km/h.

MARINE RACERS
The killer whale is the fastest recorded marine mammal. In 1956 a bull killer whale reached 55.5 km/h in the North Pacific.

LARGEST COLONY
Prairie dogs, a type of North American rodent, build enormous collective burrow networks called "towns". The largest ever recorded was discovered in 1901. It contained an estimated 400 million black-tailed prairie dogs, and covered 61,400 sq km – almost the same size as the Republic of Ireland!

The Arabian oryx (below) is the rarest antelope. At one time only zoo animals survived. These have bred successfully and have now been returned to reserves in the Middle East.

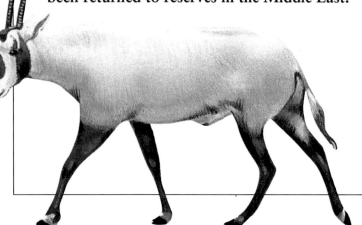

African elephants are the biggest living land mammals. An average bull elephant is over 3 m at the shoulder and weighs over 5 tonnes. A big bull weighs up to 8 tonnes. His brain weighs up to 5.5 kg. Elephants have long memories and are intelligent in many ways.

Aestivation A deep sleep that some animals go into during the summer time.

Brachiation Moving through trees by swinging by the arms from branches. Some monkeys and apes, especially gibbons, move this way.

Canine teeth The large pointed "dog teeth" at the front corners of the mouths of mammals.

Cold-blooded An animal, like a lizard, whose body temperature, and therefore its activity, depends on the warmth of its surroundings. On a hot day it can be active; on a cold day it is sluggish.

Domesticated An animal that has been tamed by humans and breeds freely in captivity. Most domestic animals were tamed when humans first began to farm the land.

Echolocation Detecting obstacles by sensing the echoes from a stream of high pitched sounds, which bounce off anything in their path. It is a way of navigating in the dark, and is used particularly by bats, whales and dolphins.

Herbivore An animal that feeds on plants.

Hibernation A deep, coma-like winter sleep. Some small animals survive the cold and lack of food during the winter by hibernating.

Home range The living area of an animal or group of animals. The edges of the area may be shared with others of the same species.

Incisor teeth The biting teeth at the front of a mammal's mouth.

Marsupial A kind of mammal, most of which live in Australia, though some, such as the opossum, are found in South and North America. The young are born underdeveloped and complete their development in a pouch on their mothers' underside, where they are fed on milk.

Molar teeth The large teeth, each with several roots, that lie in the backs of the mouths of mammals. Herbivores use them for grinding food, carnivores use them for slicing meat into pieces small enough to be swallowed.

Omnivore An animal that eats anything, like a rat, a bear or a human.

Opposable Fingers or toes that can be folded across the palm of the hand or the sole of the foot, like we can fold our thumbs, so that we can grasp things.

GLOSSARY

Species A separate kind of living thing. Normally only members of the same species are able to breed together and produce healthy offspring.

Suckling The act of feeding a baby mammal on its mother's milk.

Territory An area within the home range of a mammal or group of mammals that is defended against others of the same species.

Ultrasound Sounds of a pitch too high for human ears to hear. It is used by mammals in echolocation.

Vertebrate An animal with backbones (and other bones such as limb and skull bones). Fishes, amphibians, reptiles, birds and mammals are all vertebrates.

Warm-blooded Animals that have constant, high body temperatures, whatever the warmth or coldness of their surroundings. Unlike cold-blooded animals they are able to be active whatever the weather.

INDEX

Photo Credits